Coast Hills Women's Devotional
By: Debbie Pelichowski

Copyright © 2024 by Coast Hills Church
All rights reserved.

All biblical references in NLT unless otherwise noted.

No portion of this book may be reproduced in any form without written permission from the publisher or author, except as permitted by U.S. copyright law.

What a gift it is to put out this CTJ Devotional Book, it's been a dream of mine for many years! Here is the CTJ story…

"Cling To Jesus" has been my tagline since 2005. That's when I started sending daily Bible Verses to family and friends with 'my thoughts'… and today it has grown to over 24 text threads across the USA, WhatsApp's as far as Africa and now posted on Instagram/Facebook.

In 2020, Vinny Giovenelli came into our family and is now our daughter Sarah's husband! When he started dating 'Sissy', of course I sent him the Bible Verses, which ALWAYS ended in "Cling To Jesus"! The next time we saw Vinny he said, "Hey Debs, CTJ!" I said, "What is CTJ?" Vinny said, "CLING TO JESUS!" and it stuck!!!

So…CTJ was 'established' in 2020 from our very own Vinny!

I pray this will be a reminder to you to take your eyes off of any situation that may be causing anxiety and remember to CTJ!!!

Debbie Pelichowski
Women's Director at Coast Hills Church
Follow me at…
Instagram @dpelichowski
Facebook @debbiepelichowski

"Create in me a clean heart, O God. Renew a loyal spirit within me."

Psalm 51:10

This is King David, crying out to the Lord after making some very bad decisions! He's not denying or justifying his actions, he's owning them and he knows *only* the Lord can give him a *new* spirit.

So often we hide or explain away our actions, but we need to own them and bring them to the *only One* who can make a difference!

Own it
Confess it to Jesus
Be washed clean!

Cling to Jesus

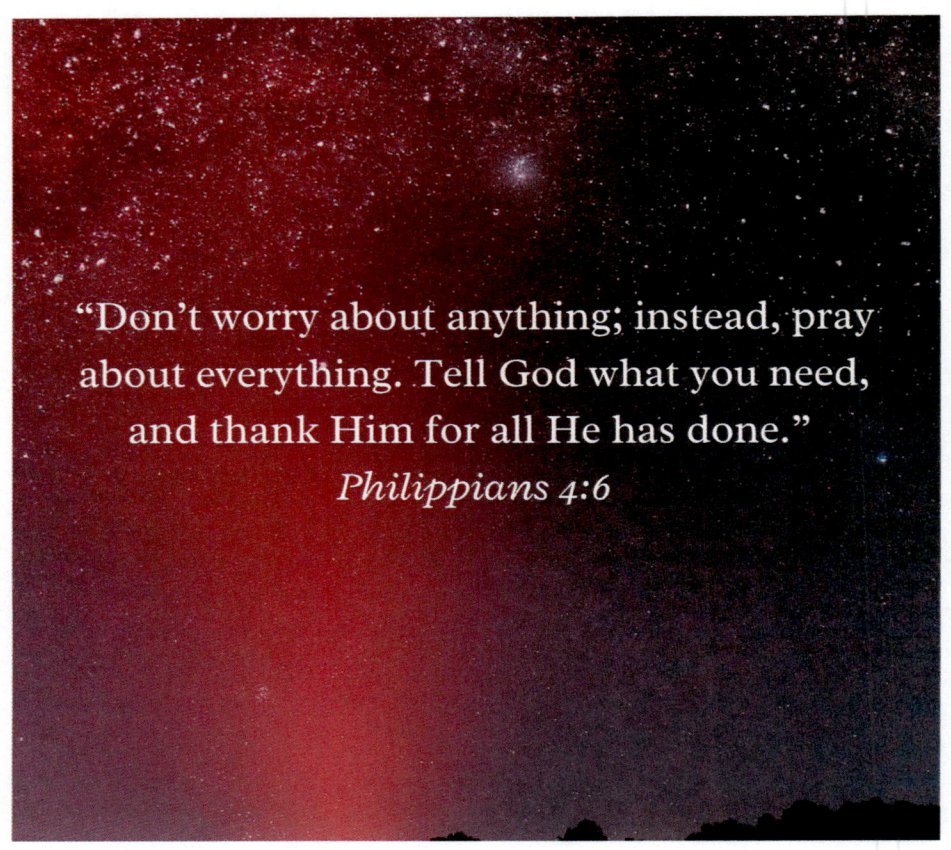

We will have worrying times. God knew it, that's why He's got this verse in here!
This side of eternity we *will* worry and have anxiety.

We need to bring it to Him.
As we sit with Him in prayer and feel His embrace all around us, we can walk through all things!

He will change us from the inside out when we come to Him.

Cling to Jesus

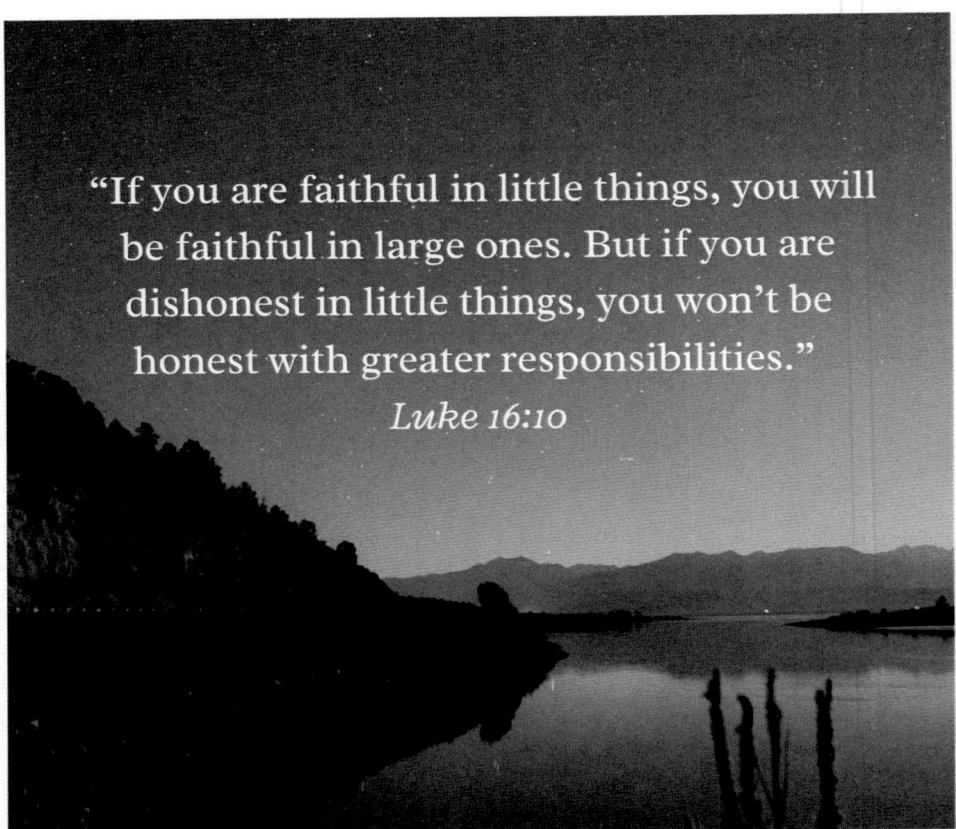

"If you are faithful in little things, you will be faithful in large ones. But if you are dishonest in little things, you won't be honest with greater responsibilities."
Luke 16:10

How are we using what the Lord has already given us? So often we get stuck—waiting for *more* to use for His Kingdom.

We need to use what He's given us today. He will take that and grow it into whatever He desires.

We are to be faithful right where we are!

Faithfully share who Jesus is in any situation. It's not dependent on what you have or where you are in your life.

Cling to Jesus

Waiting—oh, wow—waiting is so hard!
God knew it would be hard for us, so He gives us this reminder.

He's also giving us insight, I believe, when He says, "Be brave and courageous" and follows it again with "wait!"

To me this is a reminder from Him: it will get scary and frustrating, you will be anxious and fearful. Just be *brave* and courageous in *Him!*

Jesus Himself promises that this side of eternity (in this world) we will have "many trials" (John 16:33) but He tells us to *take heart*, He has overcome the world!

Cling to Jesus

Prayer doesn't instantly take away our hardships. Remember, Paul suffered a "thorn in his side" (2 Corinthians 12:7)—a hardship he prayed about that was never taken away. Unfortunately, this side of eternity we are not guaranteed a stress-free life!

But as we go through these hardships and choose to cling to Him and pray, *He* changes how we handle whatever comes our way! *He* sustains us, *He* gives us joy in Him through it all!

And let's remember, His mercies are new every morning. . .great is His faithfulness (Lamentations 3:23)! Praise Him on the mountain tops and in the valleys!

Cling to Jesus

"I tell you the truth, those who listen to my message and believe in God who sent me have eternal life. They will never be condemned for their sins, but they have already passed from death into life."
John 5:24

These are Jesus' words! Believe in Him and have eternal life! Once you do that, your "abundant life" begins, immediately! We can have that abundant life with Him *here*, this side of eternity!

Are you accessing His gift—the abundant life He has promised? Even in hard circumstances?

We were never promised an easy life here. . .but we can have an abundant, joy-filled life no matter what the circumstance as we rely on His Holy Spirit and cling to Jesus.

Cling to Jesus

"When anxiety was great within me, your consolation brought me joy."
Psalm 94:19 (NIV)

Anxiety, this side of eternity, is a certain thing! There are so many ups and downs, so many uncertainties, fears, concerns, hurt—the list goes on and on, which brings on anxiety.

But God:
His consolation is our hope!
My hope is in the joy of *the Lord,*
He is my strength,
He is my anchor,
He will never leave,
His love is unending,
I can be free indeed, free *in Him!*

There are times in life that the Lord has even provided the amazing help of doctors to also help get through the anxieties of life. In all of it, *He* is in control!

Cling to Jesus

"Everywhere—from east to west— praise the name of the Lord."
Psalm 113:3

Everywhere and in *every* situation we are to praise the Lord!
Why? Because God is always working even if we don't feel it or see it, and His Word tells us to.

We face all kinds of trials this side of eternity. Remember, this is not our home and we live, for now, in a broken and sin-filled place.

But He is preparing our "forever home" and has given us the opportunity to be in a real relationship with the Father. This is why we praise *always*!

Cling to Jesus

"Never speak harshly to an older man, but appeal to him respectfully as you would to your own father. Talk to younger men as you would to your own brothers. Treat older women as you would your mother, and treat younger women with all purity as you would your own sisters."

1 Timothy 5:1–2

It's so cool that God, from the beginning, spoke about the importance of multi-generational gatherings!

I believe a church or any organization filled with all young people or all older people is missing out. We can gain wisdom from each other, young and old.

The younger have zeal, excitement, and energy. The older have wisdom, compassion, and have lived a life that can be learned from—good and bad.

So take an opportunity today to reach out to someone younger or older. Grab coffee, go for a walk. Enjoy the gifts that each of you can bring to the other!

Cling to Jesus

"Study this Book of Instruction continually. Meditate on it day and night so you will be sure to obey everything written in it. Only then will you prosper and succeed in all you do."

Joshua 1:8

This Book of Instruction is the Bible. There is a plan for this life, and our plan is in God's Word, the Bible!

So, meditate on His Word. Open your Bible, read, listen and ask the Holy Spirit to help you live it out!

We do not "meditate" in the same way the world does. Instead, biblical meditation is prayerfully focusing our minds on the Lord and His Word.

Prospering and succeeding is not referring to comfort or perfection on this earth. No, this side of eternity will be tough. (Jesus even reminds us of this in John 16:33.)

But Heaven waits! That's where we will experience absolute comfort and succeed in perfectly doing the good we want to do.

Cling to Jesus

As you woke up, maybe the worries of this life flooded your mind. I know they do at times for me.

We need to be "on guard!" We need to look away from the fearful unknown and look to the *only* one who can see us through—our Lord!

Stand firm in your faith, knowing who God is and relying on His Holy Spirit— then you can be courageous and strong!

Cling to Jesus

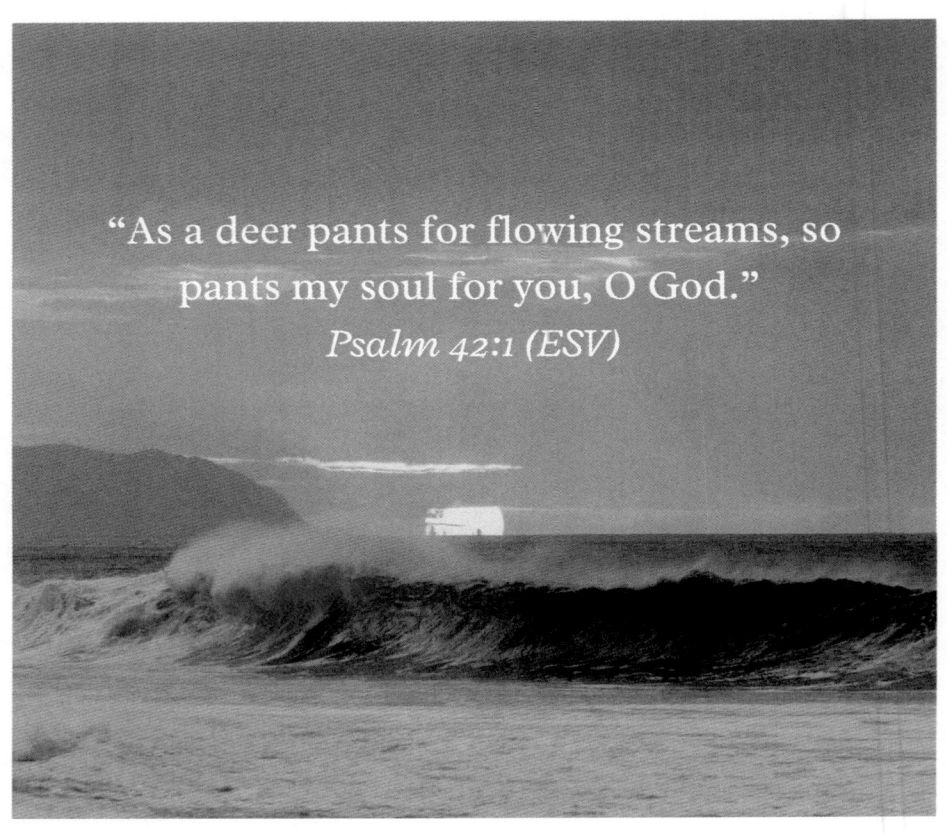

"As a deer pants for flowing streams, so pants my soul for you, O God."
Psalm 42:1 (ESV)

The Psalmist here has been thought to be in complete desperation, even possibly depressed. Yet this is how he chooses to walk this out: by clinging to God, longing *only* for God, looking to God for his "living water!"

Even when we are in pain—when we are feeling alone and depressed—this reminds us what we need to do. We need to desperately run to Him, to cry out to Him, and He will see us through.

He will take us through it—not around or beside it—but through it, carrying us along the way.

He will be the streams of Living Water (John 7:38) that we need!

Cling to Jesus

"We love each other because He loved us first."

1 John 4:19

We need to love because *He first* loved us!

This will show the world you are different—when you choose to love in any situation, especially if it's an unlovable situation.

I've wrestled with this and I'll be honest—I don't want to show love if I've been hurt.
But then God reminds me from His Word to *love*.

Jesus loves us so much and He chose to die for us *when we were unlovable.*

This kind of love is not possible without the Holy Spirit living in us—and even with Him, it's a struggle and a process. But as with all things, nothing is impossible for God!

Cling to Jesus

"Give, and you will receive. Your gift will return to you in full—pressed down, shaken together to make room for more, running over, and poured into your lap. The amount you give will determine the amount you get back."
Luke 6:38

When we read "give," so often we go right to the giving of our finances. I believe this is part of what Jesus is saying—but not all.

How we live with people is just as important. Are we giving mercy and forgiveness?
We can live giving all our finances away, but if we do not give love, mercy and forgiveness to others—and not just other believers, but to all—we will come up empty!

We give because Jesus gave to us: undeserved love, mercy, grace and forgiveness.

Let's give love in this way. It will be poured back into us, overflowing, from our Savior!

Cling to Jesus

"I waited patiently for the Lord to help me, and He turned to me and heard my cry. He lifted me out of the pit of despair, out of the mud and the mire. He set my feet on solid ground and steadied me as I walked along."

Psalm 40:1-2

Wait on the Lord!

He is there, He hears us, He sees us, He never leaves us, no matter what we are going through. As we walk through things this side of eternity, it will be—at times— like we are walking in a "pit of despair," sinking in the mud and mire.

Wait on *Him!*
If we are surrendered to Jesus, He has set us on *solid ground.*

This side of eternity, there will be hard times. We need to wait—wait on *Him* and look to see all He wants to teach us in the hard times!

Cling to Jesus

"So be strong and courageous, all you who put your hope in the Lord!"
Psalm 31:24

This is King David crying out to the Lord at a time in his life that everyone is against him. Even his son is trying to kill him and he's desperate.

He reminds himself: *God* never leaves us, no matter what things look like around us!

The Lord is there and we can take courage in *Him*.

He will never leave or forsake us!
We can put *all* our hope in Him.

Cling to Jesus

This phrase, "be strong and courageous" comes up over and over in the Old Testament.

Why? Because God knew we needed to hear this over and over!

In this passage, King Asa encouraged God's people to get rid of all their idols. He knew they would need this reminder as they let go of the "things of this world"(1 John 2:15) that were dragging them down.

We need this verse just as much. Look around—it's scary and He's still saying, "be *strong* and *courageous*"!

Cling to Jesus

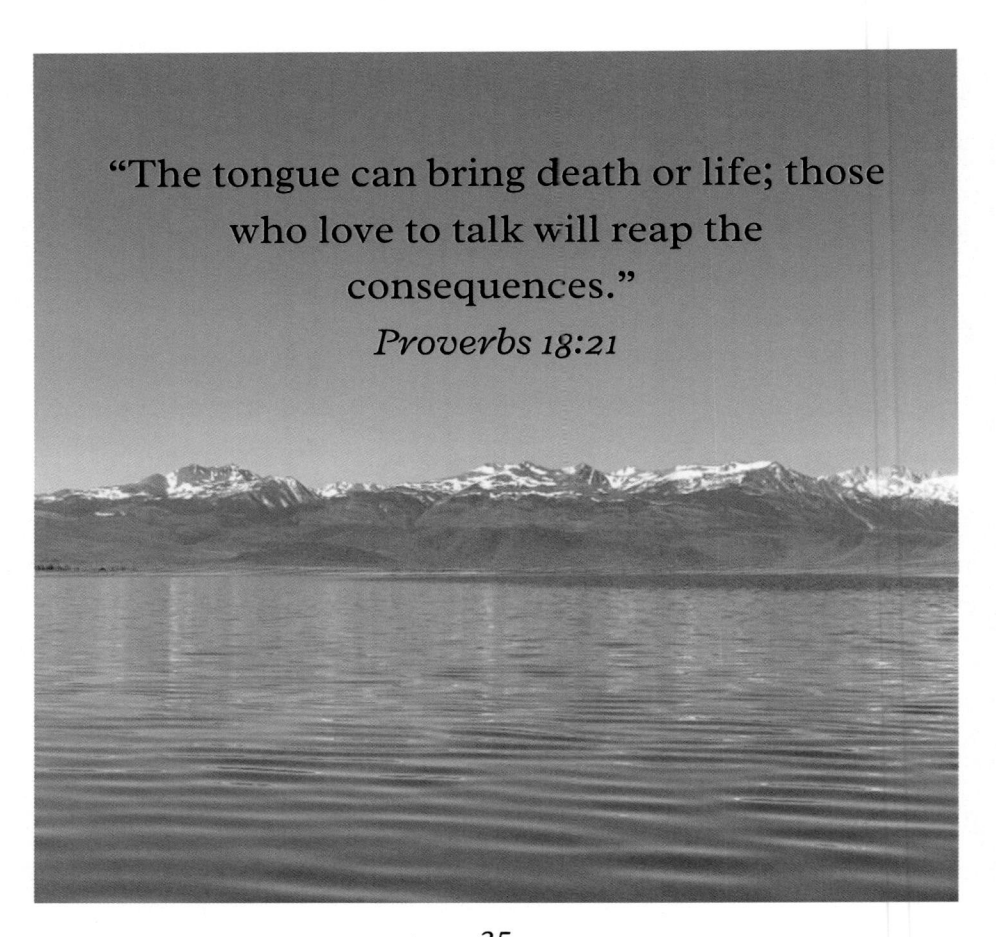

"The tongue can bring death or life; those who love to talk will reap the consequences."

Proverbs 18:21

We can speak *life* or *death* into someone!

How do you speak to others?

None of us get it right all the time, but do you lift others up or tear them down?

Are you a "life- giving" person with your words, or a "toxic person"?

Our tongues are *powerful*. Choose to use yours to lift up and bring life, not tear down!

How do we do this? By clinging to Jesus!

Cling to Jesus

"Stay alert! Watch out for your great enemy, the devil. He prowls around like a roaring lion, looking for someone to devour. Stand firm against him, and be strong in your faith. Remember that your family of believers all over the world is going through the same kind of suffering you are."
1 Peter 5:8–9

Satan is real. We have a real enemy!
This enemy wants to devour, kill and destroy —
especially those who believe in Jesus, those who
believe that He is the *way*, the *truth*, and the *life*,
the only way to the Father (John 14:6).

This passage reminds us to stay alert and stand
firm. Jesus battled Satan in the wilderness and He
used Scripture to stand firm (Luke 4:1-13).

The way we stand firm against the enemy is by
knowing truth. The Bible has that truth, and that
truth will set us free (John 8:32) and give us the
ability to *stand firm!*

Cling to Jesus

"Love means doing what God has commanded us, and He has commanded us to love one another, just as you heard from the beginning."

2 John 1:6

This is a command, not a suggestion!

We need to walk in love. We need to choose to love one another—even the "one anothers" who may be a bit hard to love, or the ones who don't love you back.

His command is to *love*. . .period!

How can we do this?
Only with His help!

Cling to Jesus

"Share each other's burdens, and in this way obey the law of Christ."
Galatians 6:2

This is just another reminder that we are *not* to walk through this life alone!

Sharing each other's burdens is a good thing. For me, it's easier to help you with your burden than to let someone help me —but we need to let others help when we need help.

Don't rob them of the blessing that helping truly is!

Keep close to Jesus, asking *Him* what burdens you should pick up.

At times we try to carry things He never intended us to carry. Be wise!

Cling to Jesus

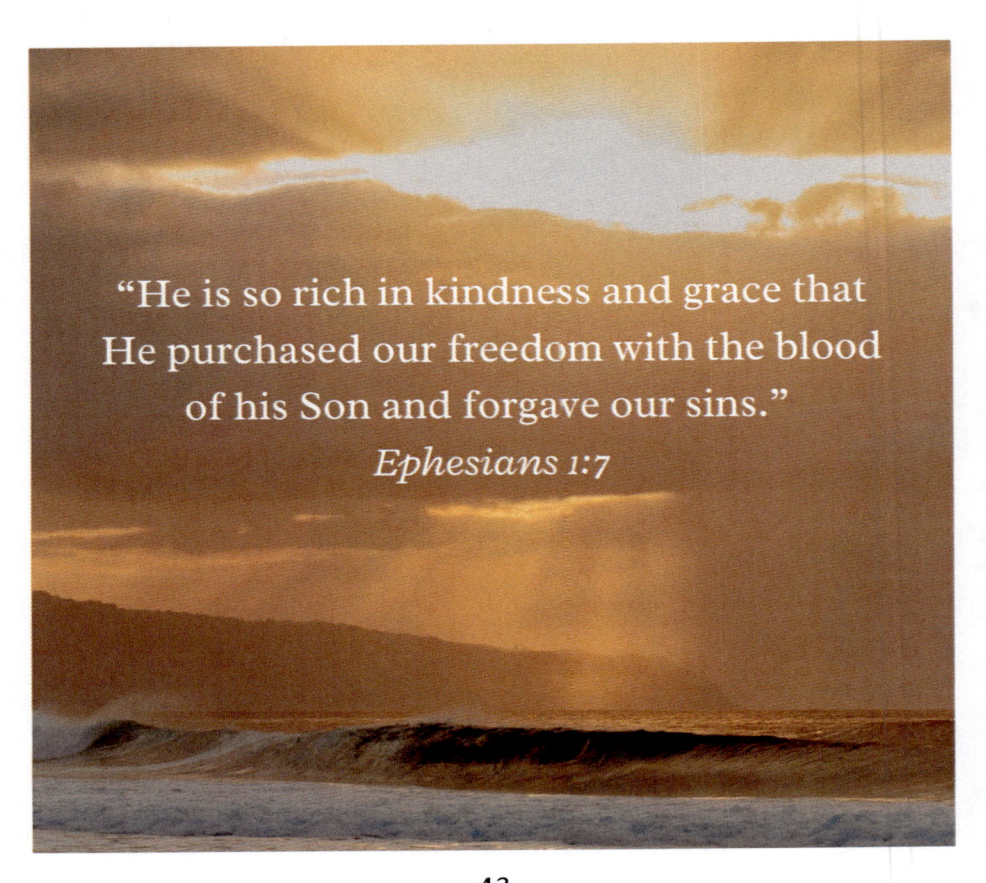

> "He is so rich in kindness and grace that He purchased our freedom with the blood of his Son and forgave our sins."
>
> *Ephesians 1:7*

This is who our Lord is, filled with kindness, grace and love! We are free and forgiven in Him once we've surrendered to Jesus. One of our problems is not being able to accept His forgiveness. We don't feel worthy and we are *not* worthy!

We need to receive His forgiveness, given not because of anything *we've* done, but because of all *He's* already done.

Satan wants to keep us living in shame and guilt, not receiving the Lord's love and forgiveness. Don't give him that foothold!

Accept the Lord's free gift and live in the only real freedom we have: *freedom in Jesus!*

Cling to Jesus

"Worry weighs a person down; an encouraging word cheers a person up."

Proverbs 12:25

Worry does weigh us down, but we are told Jesus' burden is light (Matthew 11:28–30).

We need to go to Jesus and give Him our worries, our anxieties, our depression, and our "weight."

Jesus also showed us how He lived in community: the Father, the Son and the Holy Spirit. We need to live in community as well.

Be open and vulnerable with someone so that they can offer that encouraging word!

Be open with someone so that they will know they are not alone!

Be open with someone because the Lord meant for us to live in "real and right relationships" with Him and each other!

Cling to Jesus

"Even there your hand will guide me, and your strength will support me."
Psalm 139:10

Oh my, what a great reminder!
This is King David, recognizing God is everywhere.

Even there, His hand will guide you!

Even there, He will strengthen and support you!

I don't know where your "even there" is, but God does and He's reminding you that *even there*—in your hurt, your pain, your disappointment—He is there!

Cling to Jesus

"All praise to God, the Father of our Lord Jesus Christ. God is our merciful Father and the source of all comfort. He comforts us in all our troubles so that we can comfort others. When they are troubled, we will be able to give them the same comfort God has given us."

2 Corinthians 1:3-4

I love this reality. When we suffer this side of eternity, our Lord will comfort us and use it for *His* glory as we walk others through the same sufferings!

Nothing is wasted in His economy. The question is, are we willing to allow Him to work in and through us in that suffering? I pray we are.

I've seen firsthand how powerful that can be, not just for others but for us as well.

This side of eternity we will have suffering. But take heart, Jesus *overcame* the world (John 16:33)!

Cling to Jesus

> "O people, the Lord has told you what is good,
> and this is what He requires of you:
> to do what is right, to love mercy,
> and to walk humbly with your God."
> *Micah 6:8b*

This statement is from God to the people of Israel, through the Prophet Micah.

The people—*again*—were grumbling, saying "God, you expect too much!"

And this verse is how God responded to them, with what *He* really wants and how *He* wants us to live!

Easy peasy—*do* what is right, *love* mercy, and *walk* humbly before Him.

Don't overcomplicate things. We *know* right from wrong, so we need to act on it.

Show others mercy, remembering the mercy that has been given to *you!*

Walk humbly before God, asking Him to work in you through His Holy Spirit to live this out!

Cling to Jesus

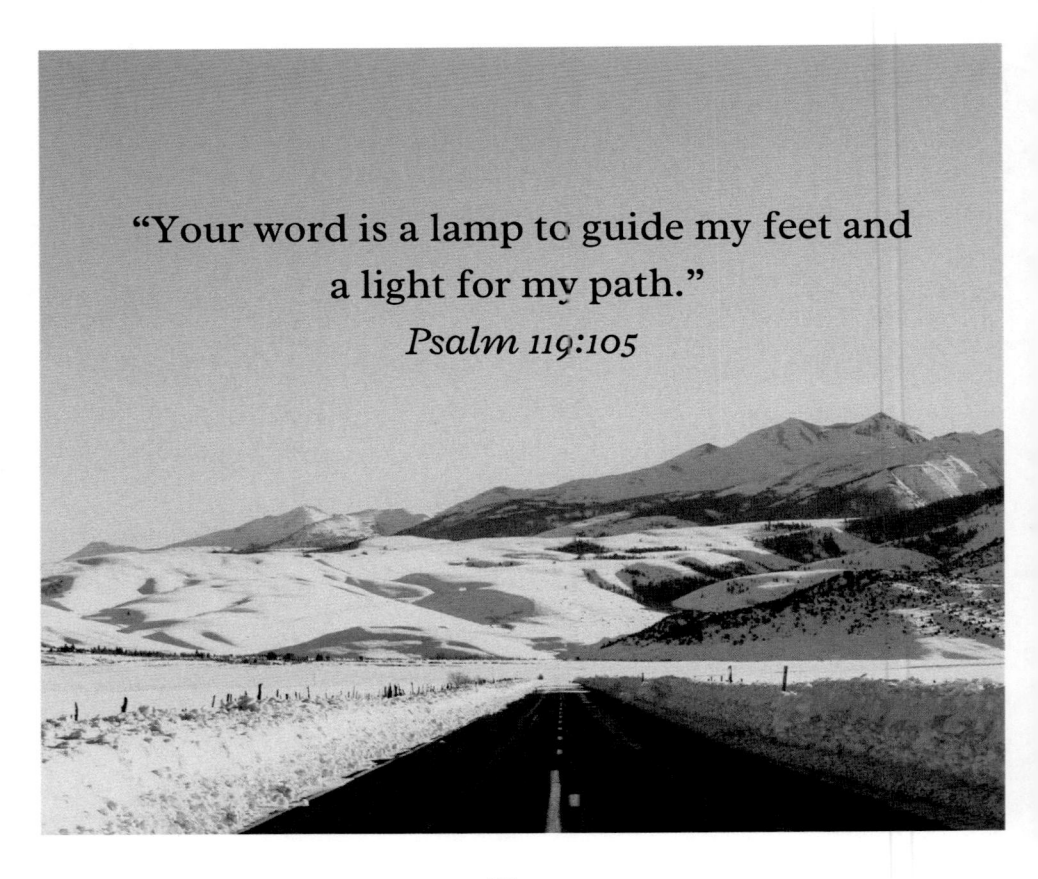

> "Your word is a lamp to guide my feet and a light for my path."
>
> *Psalm 119:105*

His Word, truly, is a lamp to my feet! My day is empty and even more chaotic and unsettling without His Word. I *need* His guidance!

At times, just opening the Bible can seem overwhelming. I encourage you to simply ask Him in! If you are His kid, His Holy Spirit lives in you and is there saying, "I will guide you through. Cling to my Spirit and I will open your eyes to what I have for you!"

If you've never surrendered your life, today is that day!
His Word *will* guide you through life this side of eternity!

Cling to Jesus

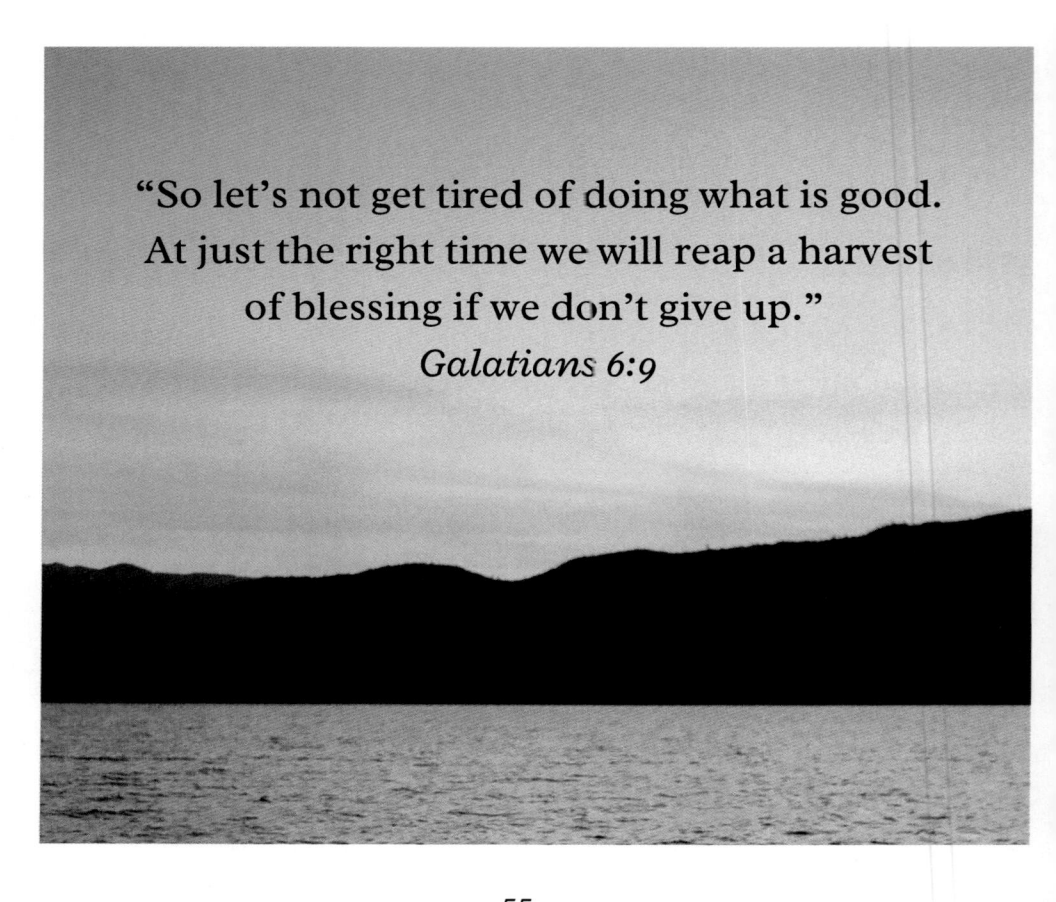

"So let's not get tired of doing what is good. At just the right time we will reap a harvest of blessing if we don't give up."
Galatians 6:9

What is the "good" Paul is talking about? The "good" is what is guided by the *Holy Spirit*. He produces the "fruit" of the Spirit (Galatians 5:22–23).

The good is not a self-motivated good that will bring us glory. It's a good brought on by the Spirit that brings *all* the glory to God!

We can't live this on our own.

Cling to Jesus

> "Great is his faithfulness; His mercies begin afresh each morning."
>
> *Lamentations 3:23*

This reminds us that no matter how far we are from the Lord or how deep we may have spiraled, God is always there! He will *never* leave us or forsake us. His mercies are new *every* morning!

If you are His, nothing can snatch you from His hands (John 10:28–29).

This is from a biblical book of "laments" called Lamentations. The author—the prophet Jeremiah—is grieving how far Israel has fallen. But God reminds us through this prophet that the Lord's mercies are new *every* morning!

Cling to that.

Cling to Jesus

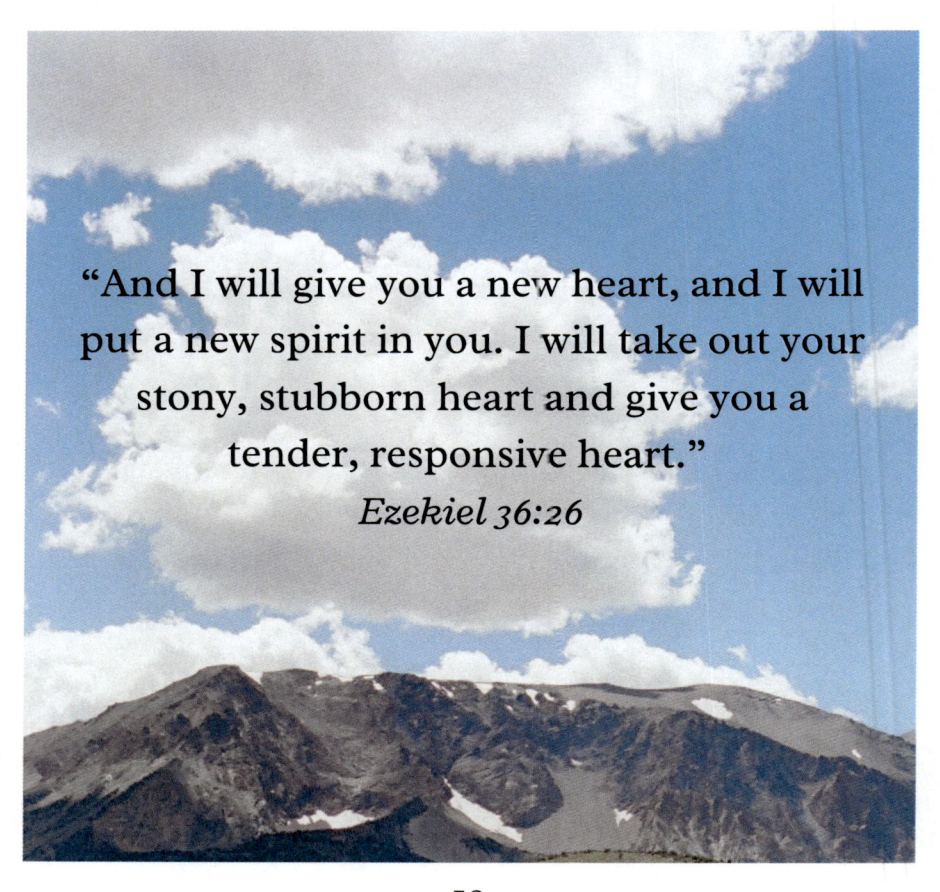

"And I will give you a new heart, and I will put a new spirit in you. I will take out your stony, stubborn heart and give you a tender, responsive heart."

Ezekiel 36:26

The Lord will give us this new heart!

Only *His* Spirit in us can change our hearts and take them from stony and stubborn to tender and loving.

When we walk through the difficulties of this life, *if* we give Him our hearts, He will give us a tender, responsive heart and use our difficulties to love and care for others!

Cling to Jesus

> "We destroy arguments and every lofty opinion raised against the knowledge of God, and take every thought captive to obey Christ."
>
> *2 Corinthians 10:5 (ESV)*

Take captive *every* thought! We need to remember this. We can not trust our everyday thoughts—the thoughts that just pop in!

There is a battle going on around us and Satan loves to whisper lies into our thoughts! Remember Eve in the Garden? He suggests little twisted thoughts. He even takes God's Word, twisting it just a little, and then we are *listening to lies!*

Taking our thoughts "captive" and taking them to the Lord is so important!
Knowing the truth of God's Word is even more important. The more we *know* Him and His Word, the less Satan can twist around!

Cling to Jesus

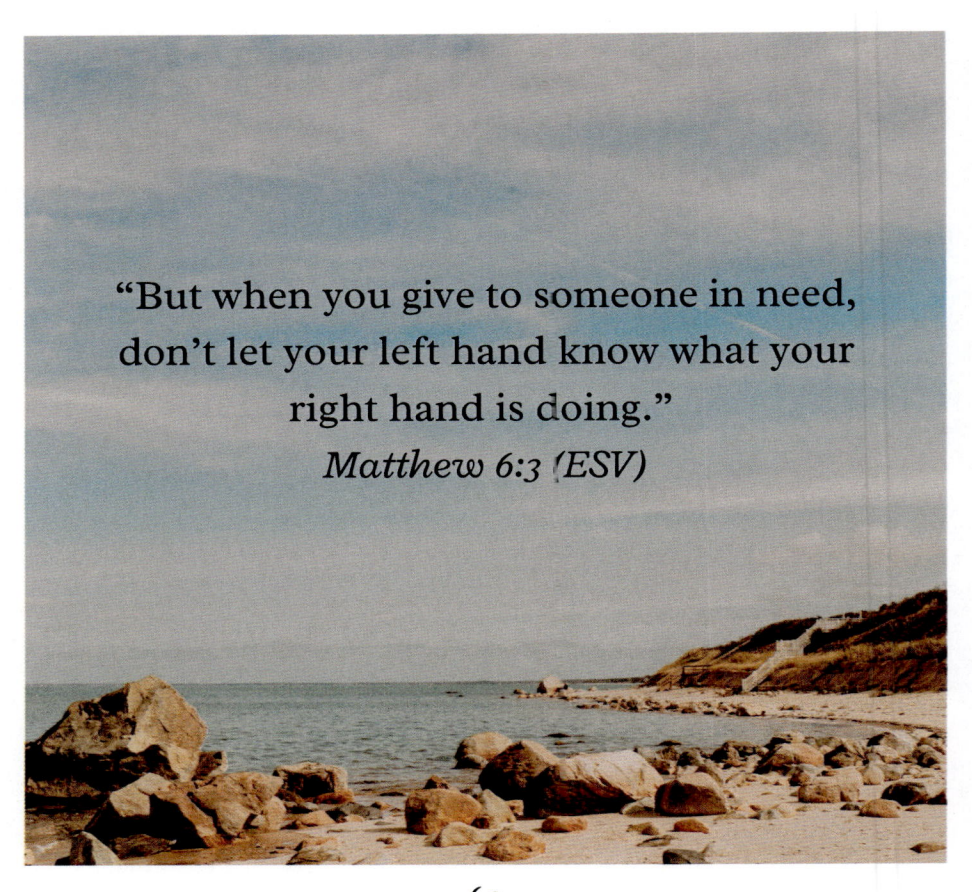

"But when you give to someone in need, don't let your left hand know what your right hand is doing."
Matthew 6:3 (ESV)

When you give, when you help those around you in need, watch your motive!

Don't give to be seen.

Don't do things for others to elevate who you are.

Do it out of pure love and devotion to the Father and the care you have for His kids, *not* for what it could bring you.

This is why Jesus says this. Keep it between you and Him!

Cling to Jesus

> "If a man has a hundred sheep and one of them wanders away, what will he do? Won't he leave the ninety-nine others on the hills and go out to search for the one that is lost?"
>
> *Matthew 18:12*

This is Jesus speaking. This is a reminder—He will pursue everyone! And *He* knows the one who has wandered away. His desire is to bring that one back!

Are you that *one*? If so, He's pursuing you. Simply surrender!

Do you know one who is wandering? Reach out and remind them you are there for them but more importantly, He is!

Cling to Jesus

"The Lord is my strength and shield. I trust Him with all my heart. He helps me, and my heart is filled with joy. I burst out in songs of thanksgiving."

Psalm 28:7

This is King David praising the Lord, who has delivered him from his enemies.

The Lord is our strength and shield. He strengthens us in the middle of chaos and covers us with His shield!

This side of eternity, it will be hard. But we are in the safety of the "palm of His hands" (John 10:28-29).

When we are His, if He allows it, He will walk us through it!

Cling to Jesus

> "That is why I tell you not to worry about everyday life—whether you have enough food and drink, or enough clothes to wear. Isn't life more than food, and your body more than clothing?"
>
> *Matthew 6:25*

Worry! We all worry about all sorts of things, from our clothes and food to our relationships and health.

Yet God's Word reminds us that:
He is in the details.
He will provide all we need.
He has a plan.
He is *always* here for each of us.

We need to put our hope *in Him*, not the things of this world (1 Timothy 6:17).
Our life in Him is way more important than the things of this world!

Cling to Jesus

"But—When God our Savior revealed His kindness and love, He saved us, not because of the righteous things we had done, but because of His mercy. He washed away our sins, giving us a new birth and new life through the Holy Spirit."

Titus 3:4b-5

We are saved through His sacrifice, His kindness, and His love, not because of anything in us!

God our Father sent His Son to this earth to save us, and He left the Holy Spirit to be our guide and counselor, living in us (1 Corinthians 6:19).

When we surrender to this truth, and accept Jesus as our Savior and Lord, we *are* born again and are daily being transformed (sanctified) into what He, our Lord, has for us (2 Peter 1:3–4).

Surrender, and. . .

Cling to Jesus

"'For the mountains may move and the hills disappear, but even then my faithful love for you will remain. My covenant of blessing will never be broken,' says the Lord, who has mercy on you."

Isaiah 54:10

I don't know the mountains you are facing in life right now, but God does. This life has so many ups and downs that we can't count on anything but change this side of eternity.

We *can* count on Him! He will never fail or let us down.

Come to Him—He wants to walk you through everything you encounter. Don't face those mountains alone!

Cling to Jesus

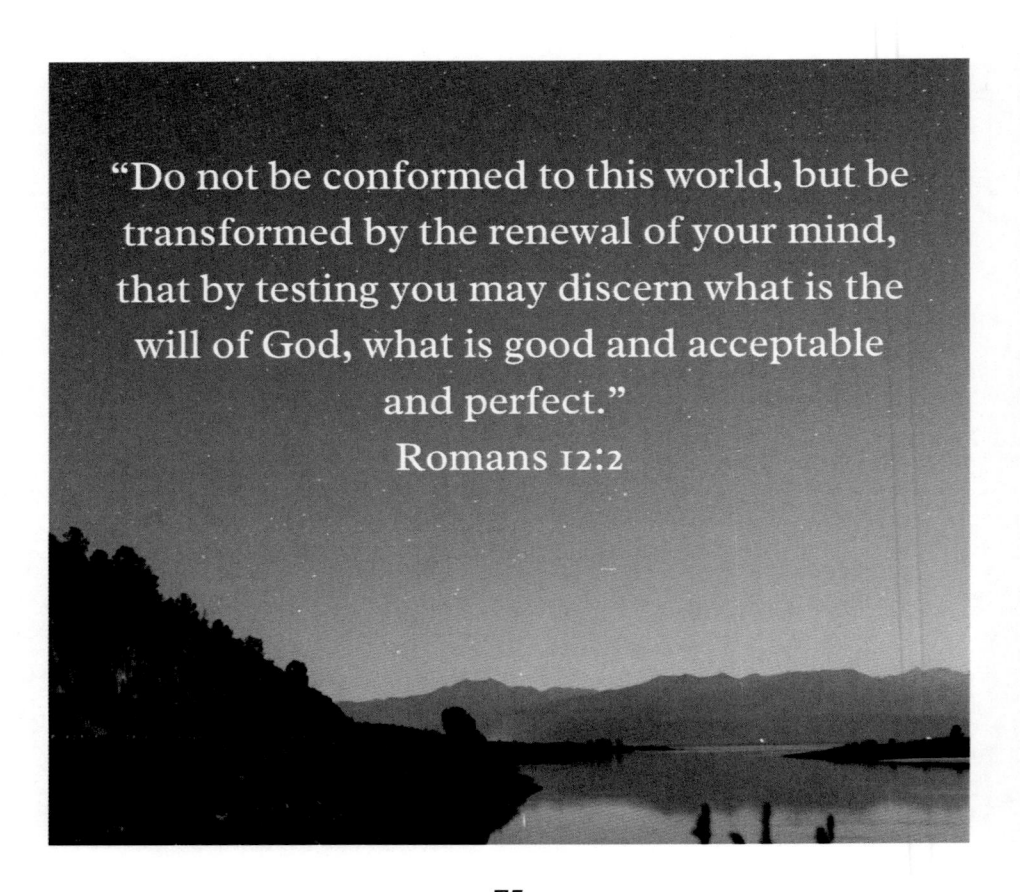

"Do not be conformed to this world, but be transformed by the renewal of your mind, that by testing you may discern what is the will of God, what is good and acceptable and perfect."

Romans 12:2

Abide with Him (John 15:9).

If we want to be different from those controlled by thoughts and pursuits of this "world,"(Matthew 6:31–33) we need to *"renew" our minds in God.*

The only way that is possible is by abiding in Him, surrendering to Him, choosing His path—the narrow one—and *not* the world's!

Listen to His Holy Spirit in you today as you abide in Him and His Word!

Cling to Jesus

> "This is my commandment: Love each other in the same way I have loved you."
> *John 15:12*

How does Jesus love?

Fully, with everything He has!

Intensely! He loved us so much He died for us (Romans 5:8).

This is the command for us—His disciples, His followers—to *love* in this way.

We can only do this in the power of His Holy Spirit!

Cling to Jesus

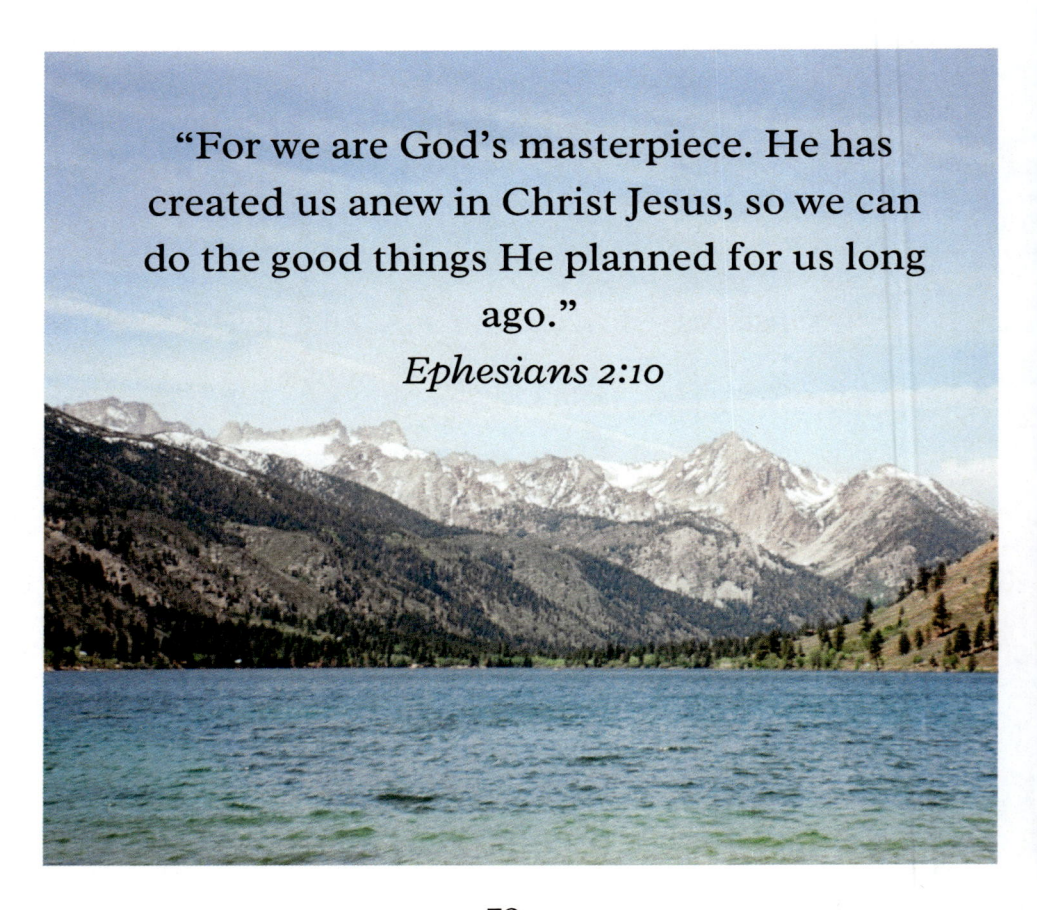

> "For we are God's masterpiece. He has created us anew in Christ Jesus, so we can do the good things He planned for us long ago."
>
> *Ephesians 2:10*

We are His masterpieces! I don't know about you but that brings me comfort, knowing He's got things covered.

When we are His—His surrendered children, listening to Him, ready to be used by Him—He's got *great* plans!

I don't know where you are in life right now, but remember, your Heavenly Father created you and He doesn't make mistakes!

Cling to that.

Cling to Jesus

81

Thank you

I could NOT have done ANY of this without the LOVE and GUIDANCE of our LORD and Savior JESUS Christ...HE is my everything and I'm so thankful HE pursued me and called me, and I finally surrendered to HIM in 1983, and I am now HIS daughter!

Thank you to my sweet husband of 44 years, Dave, your love and encouragement means everything! My kids, Danny, Stacy, Brian, Aubry, Sarah, Vinny AND my 8 amazing grandkids, Moriah, Bellah, Anna, Jeremiah, Micah, Noah, Logan and Everett...you all complete my life 'this side of eternity'! My sister Lori, the strongest woman I know and one of my BIGGEST cheerleaders!

My church family at Coast Hills Church, I'm so thankful for each of you, especially my Women's Life 'Sisters IN Christ' you mean the world to me!

Also, so thankful for the support of our Senior Pastor Jason Huffman, thank you for allowing me to be me!

Special thanks to:
Erika Pizzo, for your encouragement in this project and your knowledge of HOW to do it! THIS would not have happened without your love and encouragement!
Nancy Kington, for your editing eye, still allowing me to be me!
Anne Caringella, for your incredible talent and eye for details.
Sarah Giovenelli, MY sweet, amazing, talented daughter! The LORD has gifted you with many gifts, photography being one of them! Thank you for sharing your heart through the lens of your camera!
Sarah's website: www.thiswildromance.com - Instagram: @sarahgiovenelli

Made in the USA
Middletown, DE
30 November 2024